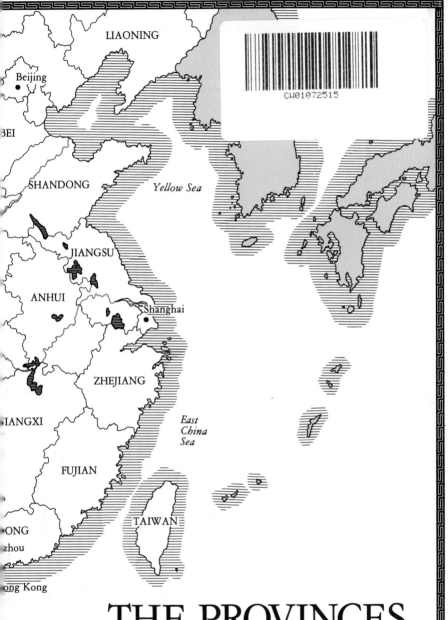

LIAONING

Beijing

BEI

SHANDONG

Yellow Sea

JIANGSU

ANHUI

Shanghai

ZHEJIANG

East
China
Sea

JIANGXI

FUJIAN

TAIWAN

ONG

zhou

ong Kong

China Sea

THE PROVINCES
OF CHINA

At the Chinese Table

T. C. LAI

HONG KONG
OXFORD UNIVERSITY PRESS
OXFORD NEW YORK
1984

Oxford University Press

Oxford London New York Toronto
Kuala Lumpur Singapore Hong Kong Tokyo
Delhi Bombay Calcutta Madras Karachi
Nairobi Dar es Salaam Cape Town
Melbourne Auckland

and associated companies in
Beirut Berlin Ibadan Mexico City Nicosia

OXFORD is a trademark of Oxford University Press.

ISBN 0 19 583841 6

Printed in Hong Kong by New Kwok Hing Printing Press Co. Ltd.
Published by Oxford University Press, Warwick House, Hong Kong

Preface

COMPARE a hungry workman consuming tripe noodles in soup from a chipped bowl at a formica-topped folding table on a street food stall with an elaborately bedecked wedding guest toying with her table napkin as she awaits her portion of shark's fin soup to be ladled by the waiter into a tiny bowl resting in a silver holder. What do they have in common? Both are 'at the Chinese table', but at very different tables, and in very different circumstances.

Yet the two examples serve to illustrate the diversity of the subject. This book is by no means an exhaustive study of the Chinese table, but is rather a brief look at it from a number of different angles.

The Chinese table is in many ways the meeting point of the varied aspects of the book: a historical survey of Chinese food and eating habits, the characteristics of Chinese food and the ingredients and cooking methods used to make what is eventually consumed at table, and the many different styles of Chinese table from the home and the restaurant to the banquet.

The food of any nation is an aspect of its culture. No people, with the exception perhaps of the French, take such an interest in, and derive such enjoyment from eating as the Chinese, with the result that food is a very major aspect of Chinese culture. The depiction of foodstuffs in art and the artistry devoted to the manufacture of table utensils point to the influence of Chinese food on art, another major aspect of Chinese culture, and for this reason reproductions of Chinese works of art have been chosen to illustrate the book.

Acknowledgements

THE author and publishers would like to thank the following for their help in providing illustrations: Mr Peter Lam, Assistant Curator of the Art Gallery, The Chinese University of Hong Kong; Mr Hugh Moss; The Hong Kong Museum of Art; and the National Palace Museum, Taipei.

Contents

I

Chinese Food in History

LEGEND has it that fire was invented and first used for cooking in China by a certain Sui Ren. Realizing that his companions were suffering stomach and intestinal ailments from eating raw food, Sui Ren bored the branch of a tree to produce fire, and cooked on it. The people enjoyed cooked food, grew healthier and gave Sui Ren his name, which means Firewood Man.

Fire was probably used for cooking in China as early as the Pleistocene period, when Peking Man (460,000–230,000 BC) lived on game meat, mostly that of a deer with thick antlers, and on wild plants such as huckleberry. Documentary evidence of the food eaten in ancient China has been found from excavations and in literature. Excavations at Banpo cun in Shaanxi province, a site of the Yangshao culture which flourished from about 5000 BC, yielded remains of foxtail millet. The *Shi Jing* (*Book of Songs*), brought together about 600 BC, mentions more than forty plants and vegetables, such as melon, gourd, turnip, leek, lettuce, mustard greens, garlic, amaranth and bamboo shoot.

A vivid description of food is contained in two poems from the *Chu Ci* (*Songs of Chu*), which date from about the fourth century BC. Both poems are summons to the soul to return to the body, as it was believed that a person's soul could leave his body while he was still alive, producing symptoms of illness, melancholy or madness. The poet lists some earthly attractions in an attempt to lure back the soul:

O soul, come back! Why should you go far away?
All your household have come to do you honour; all kinds of good food are ready:

Rice, broom-corn, early wheat, mixed all with yellow millet;
Bitter, salt, sour, hot and sweet: there are dishes of all flavours.
Ribs of the fatted ox cooked tender and succulent;
Sour and bitter blended in the soup of Wu;
Stewed turtle and roast kid, served up with yam sauce;
Geese cooked in sour sauce, casseroled duck, fried flesh of the great crane;
Braised chicken, seethed tortoise, high-seasoned, but not to spoil the taste;
Fried honey-cakes of rice flour and malt-sugar sweetmeats;
Jadelike wine, honey-flavoured, fills the winged cups;
Ice-cooled liquor, strained of impurities, clear wine, cool and refreshing;
Here are laid out the patterned ladles, and here is sparkling wine.

From *Ch'u Tz'u*, *The Songs of the South*, trans. D. Hawkes (Oxford, 1959).

The other poem from the *Chu Ci* mentions foods such as pigeon, jackal, pickled pork, dog, quail, magpie and bream.

One of the principal sources of knowledge about food and eating in the Han dynasty (206 BC–AD 220) has been the discovery, in the early 1970s, of the tombs at Mawangdui on the outskirts of Changsha in Hunan province. One of the tombs contained the Countess of Dai, who died about 168 BC. Her body had been so well preserved that parts still retained their elasticity, and inside her were found $138\frac{1}{2}$ musk melon seeds. In her tomb and in two others a quantity of food remains were discovered, and other foods were mentioned on bamboo slips. These included—grains: rice, wheat, barley, glutinous millet, millet, soy bean, red lentil; seeds: hemp, malva, mustard; fruits and vegetables: pear, jujube, plum, strawberry, melon, orange, persimmon, water caltrop, lotus root, bamboo shoot, taro; animal meats: hare, dog, pig, deer, ox, sheep; bird meats: wild goose, mandarin duck, duck, bamboo chicken, chicken, pheasant, crane, pigeon, turtledove, owl, magpie, sparrow, quail, wild duck; fish: carp, crucian carp, bream, two other kinds of carp, perch; and spices: ginger, cinnamon bark, fagara, *xinyi* buds and galangal.

The bamboo slips also provide information on seasonings and cooking methods such as roasting, scalding, shallow-frying, steaming, deep-frying, stewing, salting, sun-drying and pickling. The most common main dish was stew, which is mentioned in a variety of forms: deer meat, salt fish and bamboo shoots; deer meat and taro; deer meat and small beans; chicken and gourd; crucian carp and rice; fresh sturgeon, salted fish and lotus root; dog meat and celery; crucian carp and lotus root; beef and turnip; lamb and turnip; pork and turnip; beef and sonchus (a wild grass); and dog meat and sonchus.

It was a well-established tenet by the Han dynasty that, in the art of cooking, the five flavours (sweetness, sourness, hotness, bitterness and saltiness) should be combined to achieve harmony. Mincing and thinly slicing meat and fish were also considered an essential feature of fine food. It was during the Han dynasty that such exotic edibles as grapes, alfalfa, pomegranate, walnut, sesame, onion, caraway seeds, peas, coriander and cucumber were introduced to China from beyond her western frontiers, one of the results of China's expansion in that direction.

Although the official history of the Tang dynasty (618–907) lists a number of texts on food, none has survived and therefore little is known about how Tang cuisine differed from that of the Han.

Among vegetables, spinach, rhubarb, cabbage, spring onion, leek, garlic, yam, taro, eggplant and mushroom featured in Tang cuisine. In addition to the Chinese peach, fruits included the golden yellow peaches of Samarkand which were successfully transplanted in the imperial orchards at Changan. The Chinese cherry, the plum, apricot, pear, quince, persimmon, loquat, jujube, Canton orange, tangerine, litchi, longan and banana were familiar. The table grape, imported from Central Asia, was cultivated in Shanxi province. Among nuts consumed were hazelnuts, pine nuts, chestnuts, walnuts, pistachio nuts and sesame seeds.

Meat is seldom mentioned in Tang lists, possibly because nutritionists rated meat, especially beef, poorly. One seventh-century nutritionist believed that eating the flesh of the common yellow ox was conducive to illness and that the flesh of the black ox should be avoided at all costs; a Daoist doctor emphasized the evil effects of over-indulgence in pork. Dog flesh, however, was regarded as good for the kidneys, and wild rabbit and the hump of the Bactrian camel were commonly made into stew. Among the specialities of the south, elephant was the favourite. Elephants were abundant in the south, where the natives of Guangdong feasted on their barbecued trunks, the flavour of which was compared to that of pork. The great python was also popular, finely sliced and dipped in vinegar. The lesser soft-shell turtle and the giant soft-shell turtle were both used in soups.

The many species of fowl included goose, pheasant, partridge, and even the Far Eastern peacock. The flesh of the black hen was thought to be good for the digestion, and duck soup was regarded as so beneficial that it could reconcile estranged man and wife.

Fish also formed a significant part of the Tang diet. The carp was a favourite, including the ornamental carp with golden scales, and freshwater eels were eaten, but more for their medicinal value. Among crustacea were various kinds of crab, which were eaten in many ways. Some were preserved in vinegar, and the rich yellow 'fat' was relished in the south. Shrimps were eaten, although Tang nutritionists considered them unhealthy. Oysters, mussels and squid were also available.

As for condiments and spices, ginger continued to be popular. The traditional Chinese fagara (a kind of anise-flavoured pepper) was replaced by imported black pepper, which was called 'foreign fagara'. There were various kinds of cardamom, amongst which that known as the fleshy cardamom was really the nutmeg, which was imported from the South Seas. Cloves were regarded as a breath sweetener.

True Chinese cuisine is said to have developed in the Song dynasty (960–1279). 'Cuisine' may be defined as a 'manner or style of cooking', but the development of a cuisine is made possible only by the availability of a wide variety of ingredients, and by a considerable body of cooks and eaters who are prepared to experiment with and partake of these foodstuffs, and who enjoy eating. Such a situation presented itself in Song dynasty China.

During the Song dynasty in particular, what one ate reflected one's social status. In contrast to the rich, meat-intensive diet of the wealthy, was the simple vegetarian fare eaten by mountain villagers or people too poor to afford meat. When the Song poet, Su Shi (1036–1101), was exiled to the 'barbarian south' he often had to be content with such simple food. He wrote an essay entitled 'In Praise of Dongpo's Soup', in which he describes the soup made by Dongpo: 'It did not contain fish or meat or the five flavourings, but it had a natural sweetness. His recipe was this: he took *sung* cabbage, rape-turnip, wild daikon, and shepherd's purse, and scrubbed them thoroughly to get rid of the bitter sap. First he took a bit of oil to coat the pot, then he put in the vegetables with water, along with a bit of rice and fresh ginger ... '

Despite alien incursions over parts of northern China, which began in the tenth century and culminated in the Mongol rule of the Yuan dynasty (1279–1368), the Chinese appear to have adopted little from Mongol cuisine. Mutton is mentioned frequently in Yuan dynasty dramas, but there is no evidence in literature that the Chinese consumed sheep cooked whole in the Mongol style. It is possible that finely sliced mutton is a later addition to the Chinese culinary repertoire and not the result of Mongol influence.

Upon the founding of the Ming dynasty (1368–1644), the first emperor, Hongwu (reigned 1368–98), sought to restore the ideals and forms of Chinese life which had been undermined by alien rule. These, however, were concerned more with rituals and institutions than with the preparation of food.

Meats continued to be consumed as a flavouring for vegetables rather than as the principal component of a dish. Many people avoided beef, probably for religious reasons; many found both beef and mutton too malodorous to eat. Besides such ordinary foods as hare, quail, squab and pheasant, one Ming dynasty source mentions, as standard fare, cormorant, owl, stork and crane, peacock, swallow, magpie, raven, swan, dog, horse, donkey, mule, tiger, deer, wild boar, camel, bear, wild goat, fox, wolf and many kinds of shellfish.

Whatever special foods and cooking styles the Manchus brought with them during their rule of China (Qing dynasty, 1644–1911), they do not seem to have made much of an impression on the mainstream of Chinese cuisine. Despite the extravagance of the court, there is evidence that the Qing emperors had simple tastes: Emperor Kangxi (reigned 1662–1722) liked fresh meats, plainly cooked, fish and fresh fruit; Emperor Qianlong (reigned 1736–95) ordered a menu in 1754 which contained rather ordinary dishes.

The Qing dynasty produced several literary persons who were also food connoisseurs, critics and commentators. One of these was Yuan Mei (1716–97), who retired from an official post at the age of 33 and had sufficient means to enjoy a life of leisure, owning a vast garden called Sui Yuan in Suzhou. A prolific writer and critic, his most famous work is the *Sui Yuan Shi Dan* (*Sui Yuan Cookery Book*). Yuan Mei sought flavour in food rather than extravagance.

I always say that chicken, pork, fish and duck are the original geniuses of the board, each with a flavour of its own, each with its distinctive style; whereas sea-slug and swallows-nest (despite their costliness) are commonplace fellows, with no character—in fact, mere hangers-on. I was once asked to a party given by a certain Governor, who gave us plain boiled swallows-nest, served in enormous vases, like flower-pots. It had no taste at all. The other guests were obsequious in their praise of it. But I said: 'We are here to eat swallows-nest, not to take delivery of it wholesale.' If our host's object was simply to impress, it would have been better to put a hundred pearls into each bowl. Then we should have known that the meat had cost him tens of thousands, without the unpleasantness of being expected to eat what was uneatable.

From Arthur Waley, *Yuan Mei, Eighteenth Century Chinese Poet* (London, 1956).

Chinese cuisine today is subject to numerous influences, mainly from the West. For example, mayonnaise and salad are used as a garnish for cold lobster, and Chicken and Sweetcorn Soup is made with imported, canned cream of sweetcorn. The so-called Chinese-style Tenderloin of Beef is a clear indication that tenderloin of beef presented in that manner is not indigenous.

2

Taste and Texture

'THE five tastes cloy the palate, and vitiate the sense of taste.' If the Chinese had taken to heart these words written by the philosopher, Zhuangzi, over two thousand years ago, Chinese cuisine would have been much poorer today. While the Chinese appreciated the metaphorical beauty of the words, they realized the impracticality of them. The Chinese taste buds prevailed.

Wei, which means taste, refers to the sensuous response to food. The five categories of taste are sweetness, sourness, hotness, bitterness and saltiness, which may be combined to create other tastes. According to the Chinese, each foodstuff is accompanied by a certain taste which, upon reaching the stomach, directs itself to its designated organ: sweetness enters the spleen, sourness the liver, hotness the lungs, bitterness the heart, and saltiness the kidneys. Excess of any one taste is said to injure the receiving organ.

In spite of the sophistication of Chinese cuisine, the range of vocabulary to describe tastes and their combinations is quite inadequate. Apart from the five categories of taste, there are only a handful of names for other tastes which may or may not fall under those categories. For example, the taste of liquorice is said to be *gan*; that of *foie gras* is also so called. Surely those two foods taste quite different? The taste of Superior Stock (stock made from chicken, Jinhua ham and pork) is said to be *xian*; that of crab's roe, which is quite dissimilar, is also so called. Although Jinhua ham would come under the category of saltiness, there is no way of describing its flavour other than as 'tasty'. As there is no name to describe the combination of flavours in the popular

Pottery figurines of women working in a kitchen
Tang dynasty (618–907)
From *Out of China's Earth*, China Pictorial, Beijing

A Literary Gathering, detail
Attributed to Hui Zong, Song dynasty (960–1279)
National Palace Museum, Taipei

Teacup and stand with *qingbai* glaze
Song dynasty (960–1279)
Height (of cup) 4.9 cm, (of stand) 4.4 cm
Hong Kong Museum of Art

Pot, 1966
By Lo Ch'ing (born 1948)
Collection Shuisongshi Shanfang

Yixing ware teapot in the shape of a Buddha's hand citron
By Jinfu, early twentieth century
Height 9.2 cm
K.S. Lo Collection of Teaware, Flagstaff House Museum of Teaware, Hong Kong

Yixing ware fruit and nuts
By Chen Mingyuan, early eighteenth century
Heights 1.5–6.6 cm
K.S. Lo Collection of Teaware, Flagstaff House Museum of Teaware, Hong Kong

Sifting of Tea Leaves
By Tingqua (active mid-nineteenth century)
Hong Kong Museum of Art

dish of fried half-fat, half-lean cubes of pork, it is known simply as Sweet and Sour Pork. The paucity of vocabulary in this field is a strange phenomenon.

Although most ingredients are eaten with condiments to make them more palatable, certain foodstuffs are regarded by some as self-sufficient. Crab was considered just such a case by the dramatist, poet and essayist, Li Yu (1611–80), who said of it: 'Crab is *xian* and fat, *gan* and rich; its meat is white as jade and its roe is golden. It scores highest marks for colour, flavour and taste. It needs no improvement. To try to use something to improve its taste is like holding a torch to bright sunshine or pouring water from a ladle into a river.'

Yuan Mei said something in the same vein: 'Everything has its own taste and should not be indiscriminately mixed with other things. I have seen cooks boiling chicken, duck, goose and pork together in the same pot. This makes one ingredient taste like another and the result is most uninteresting. The good cook should have an array of pots and other utensils so that each of the meats may show its individuality and the taster's palate be pleased by the variety.'

Yuan's criticism could be applied to the very expensive dish known as *Fo Tiao Qiang* (Buddha Jumping over the Wall) which was popular until quite recently. The dish consists of double-boiled thick soup containing shark's fin, abalone, Jinhua ham, *bêche-de-mer* (literally 'sea slug', and sometimes known as sea cucumber), mushroom, conpoy (a dried shellfish similar to scallop), chicken stock and other expensive ingredients. It is supposed to be so tasty that even the Buddha, a vegetarian, would find it irresistible, hence its name. It is, however, an ostentatious mixture of expensive and incongruous ingredients which results in a dish of no characteristic taste.

As garlic predominates in French cooking, tomato in Italian, and curry in South-east Asian, soy sauce is indispensable as a flavouring agent in Chinese cooking. Made from the soy bean, soy sauce is commonly believed to be the oldest condiment known to man, although it may owe its origin to sauces made with fish or game. When seafood, meat or soy beans are salted or immersed in a mixture of salt and rice wine (or water) their protein is broken down by enzymes into amino acids. These amino acids stimulate the human taste buds, and are therefore used to augment the flavours of various foods. Soy sauce is widely used today, often with the additional flavours of, for example, mushroom or shrimp's roe, and it is always present at the dining-table.

In modern physiology the sense of taste is regarded as the response to flavour. In Chinese cuisine, however, 'taste' is the response not only to flavour, but also to visual harmony. For this reason the Chinese sometimes take great pains to make certain dishes more for decoration than consumption, a habit which is sometimes carried to excess: various ingredients are assembled or sculpted to form birds, animals or flowers.

Visually, what most distinguishes Chinese food is the way in which ingredients are cut or fragmented. Chinese chefs pride themselves on their skills in the methods of preparation: ingredients may be sliced, cubed, diced, shredded or minced, the more uniformly the better. The cutting of the principal ingredient in a dish determines the shape or preparation of the others, resulting in dishes such as Chicken Cubes with Walnut, Sliced Beef with Bamboo Shoot, and Shredded Pork with Beansprouts.

Apart from taste and visual harmony, the respect for texture is an important feature of Chinese cuisine. The majority of expensive ingredients are valued almost entirely for their texture, as many are rather tasteless by themselves and depend on good stock and flavouring to make them more palatable. A number of foods eaten for their textural qualities are said to possess invigorating or aphrodisiac powers, a belief which encourages their consumption.

The texture of each ingredient is sensed by the tongue, the teeth and the throat: shark's fin is gelatinous, crunchy and slippery; abalone is rubbery, smooth and chewy; bird's nest is tender and delicate; liver is grainy; and gizzards are fibrous. To people who are not attuned to the appreciation of textures, many of these qualities are classified under the epithet 'slimy'.

Control of texture (which requires greater skill than the control of taste) is therefore an important preoccupation of a good cook, who goes to great lengths to achieve the desired quality. One of the dishes used to test an applicant for the job of chef is Stir-fried Beef Slices, which requires skill, experience and judgement to get the beef just right when served. Cooked in a very hot wok with boiling oil, the thinly sliced beef may be either underdone or overdone if it is not removed from the wok at exactly the right moment. The cook may miss it by a matter of seconds.

Another good test of culinary skill is the steaming of freshly killed fish. The timing must be precise, so that, when served piping hot, the fish is succulent and smooth, and not, as when overcooked, powdery and 'dead'.

The Chinese gourmet's delight in the texture of foods will be evident at a banquet, where he will select the pieces with textures that please him most, such as the wing or gizzard of a chicken, the head of a fish, the bladder of a good-sized steamed garoupa, the duck's tongue, the foot of a goose. The gourmet's tongue is highly disciplined. It is able to distinguish the cheek of a fish, its soft underbelly, the jelly-like tissue at the base of the dorsal fins. If it were not for the gourmet's delight in the exploration of textures, expensive ingredients such as shark's fin, bird's nest and abalone would not continue to command the exorbitant prices that they do today.

3
Food as Medicine

ALTHOUGH the office of imperial dietitian (literally 'food doctor official') was instituted about the third century BC, one of the few treatises on food as medicine to have survived is the *Yin Shan Zheng Yao* (*Principles of Correct Diet*) of 1330, by Hu Sihui, who was the imperial dietitian from 1315 to 1330, during the Yuan dynasty. A paragraph in the preface reads:

What determines human life is the mind which is the master of the body ... if the body is at ease and in harmony with its environment, the mind will be able to deal with all changes in life. Thus it is important to keep the body in good repair and maintenance, the essence of which is to keep to the golden mean, that is, not to be deficient in nutrition and not to indulge in excesses ... Use the five tastes to temper the five vital organs. If these are at peace, the vital fluid in us will flow smoothly, then our mind will find its equilibrium ... and the whole person will find himself in a state of supreme well-being.

Some of the health rules advocated by Hu Sihui may also be quoted:

Saltiness makes blood circulate faster, and is bad for people with blood disorders; sweet food is bad for muscles; sour food is bad for veins; drinking tea on an empty stomach is damaging to health; after eating hot food and perspiring, avoid draughts; after a meal, rinse the mouth with warm water to prevent bad breath and tooth decay; after a full meal do not wash your hair, avoid sex like an arrow, avoid wine like an enemy; people with heart disease should avoid saltiness and eat more small beans and dog meat.

It was originally believed that a good doctor must first make a diagnosis of his patient and, having identified the cause of a debility or disease, order him to eat certain foods. Only when food failed should the doctor prescribe medicine.

All foods are therefore considered by the Chinese to have a

remedial or curative value, and a nutritional diet should strike a balance between the two main categories of foods: those classified as 'cold', and those classified as 'hot'. In between, some foods are graded as 'cooling', 'warming', or 'neutral', and the Cantonese make a further sub-division, *bu* (literally 'supplementary', but used in the sense of 'highly tonic or nutritious'). The opposite of *bu* is *xue* (damaging).

This classification of foods has no scientific basis, and opinions on certain categorizations vary. There are, however, certain traditional ways of judging whether a food is hot or cold, depending on its taste, its method of preparation and its physical effect on the body.

Bitter foods are considered cold. Salty foods and the sourness of citrus fruits are cooling. Most beans, breads and fruits are neutral to cooling (although there are some exceptions among the fruits, such as litchis and mangoes, which are considered dry-and-hot, and wet-and-hot respectively). Honey and white sugar are cooling, whereas brown sugar is warming. Red vinegar, because of its colour, is considered warmer than white. Most meats are warming, and chilli-flavoured and spicy foods are invariably hot.

Different methods of preparation and cooking can affect the properties of an ingredient: when chilled, foods become cool; when roasted or broiled, foods become hot. Steaming does not alter the property of a raw ingredient, but deep-frying almost invariably renders a food hot.

A balanced meal should therefore include some foods that are cooling, such as vegetables, and some that are warming, such as meat, to be consumed with a good amount of neutral food such as rice.

The term *bu* applies to any food that supplements certain deficiencies in the body. Foods considered *bu* are dismissed by some as simply those rich in high-quality protein. Most are translucent, with a 'slimy' or crunchy, sometimes rubbery, texture, and little or no taste, such as shark's fin, bird's nest, *bêche-de-mer* and silver fungus. All of these require preparation and prolonged cooking, which reduces some of them to a gelatinous state indicative of the presence of easily digested high-quality protein.

The supplementary properties of an ingredient may be further reinforced with the addition of health-giving herbs such as ginseng, *qi zi* and *bei qiu*. Double-boiling in a lidded container is believed to preserve the beneficial properties of various ingredients, whereas ordinary boiling may destroy them.

There is a commonly believed theory that like affects like: in other words, eating the internal organ (such as the heart, kidney or liver) of an animal strengthens the corresponding organ in the consumer's own body. The analogy can be extended to all organs of the body.

It is difficult to prove or disprove the effectiveness of certain foods against certain ailments, as the curative process may be very slow. Between the initial ingestion of a supposedly potent ingredient and the first signs of improvement, there may be various interventions, or an ailment may take its natural course and disappear. There are countless recipes for the prevention or treatment of conditions or ailments: bird's nest, for example, is claimed to preserve a person's complexion if taken regularly over a long period of time; dried longan (dragon's eye fruit) is supposed to calm the nerves; seaweed, onions, chestnuts, and tomatoes are believed to be good for high blood pressure. One must have faith to embark on a course of Chinese preventive or curative treatment.

4
Cooking Methods

VITAL to the taste and texture of food, and to its classification as hot or cold, is the method by which it is cooked. Cooking methods depend on the control of heat, a skill that is central to the art of Chinese cooking.

The control of heat was discussed as early as the third century BC in the *Lu Shi Chun Qiu*, a history written by a certain Lu, who says that the control of fire determines success or failure in cooking, and that the fire should be regulated so that some ingredients may be cooked quickly and others slowly. Stewed dried abalone and stir-fried sliced kidney would be two extreme examples. The former requires hour upon hour of slow simmering, with the frequent addition of water to prevent scorching; the latter requires only three or four seconds of cooking over a very hot fire, in a pre-heated wok, with a few rapid strokes of the spatula.

Because of the importance attached by the Chinese to the control of heat in cooking, verbs to indicate the various cooking methods are numerous. *Zhu* is the general Chinese verb which applies to all cooking methods, only the most common of which are described here.

Some of the terms used to describe methods of boiling, simmering and stewing are *shuan*, *qin*, *quan* and *lu*. *Shuan* refers to the brief boiling of thinly sliced meat, fish and other ingredients in a hot-pot or chafing dish. A number of restaurants specialize in this method of cooking, which is performed by diners at the table.

When tenderness and complete retention of the original flavour of chicken are aimed at in cooking a whole fowl, the desired result can be obtained by the process known as *qin* (literally 'immersion'). This method of boiling and cooling is the one used by the Cantonese to cook Chicken in Superior Stock which is described on p. 24.

When tenderness cannot be achieved by the *qin* method, the *quan* method of prolonged and repeated boiling is used. The main ingredient, often beef or mutton, is fried briefly in a little oil, with the addition of various seasonings and supplementary ingredients. When the contents have been brought to the boil the heat is reduced, and the meat left to simmer and then cool. The processes of boiling, simmering and cooling are then repeated several times.

The process known as *lu*, used to give meat, entrails and poultry a strong aromatic flavour, is unique to the Chinese, and is particularly popular with the Cantonese. Sugar, soy sauce, ginger, Shaoxing (or Yellow) wine and five-spice powder are used to prepare the stock in which the principal ingredient is simmered for hours until the flavours have been assimilated. This 'original stock' is reused to become the 'master stock', which is then reused again and again, and enriched with each addition of fresh ingredients.

The Cantonese also pride themselves on their technique of steaming, *zheng*, which helps to retain the 'original' taste and firm, yet tender, texture of fish. Only freshly killed fish qualifies for this process, and experience and good timing are essential for success (see p. 23). Steaming is common in daily cooking, and small quantities of ingredients are often spread thinly on a utensil to be cooked over steaming rice.

When ingredients are steamed in a closed receptacle, the process is known as *dun*. Usually the steaming is prolonged, ranging from two to six hours. Medicinal herbs are often added as the resulting fluid is generally taken as a tonic.

Of the various methods of frying, *zha* (deep-frying) is much the same in Chinese as in Western cuisines. However, *chao* (stir-frying or quick-frying) is a Chinese invention. The ingredients to be cooked are usually cut into small cubes or strips which are subjected to rapid stirring in a small amount of oil in the wok, so that their surfaces are quickly and evenly exposed to the heat. Stir-fried dishes are expected to be consumed with alacrity, to allow the diners to enjoy the flavour, taste and, even more important, the *huo qi* (vital essence) which the Chinese connoisseur prizes very highly. Another form of stir-frying known as *bao* (literally 'explosive frying') requires the oil to be fiercely hot and the cooking process to be very brief indeed.

Variations on the methods discussed are many, and all are represented by terms which are readily understood by those with an interest in Chinese cooking.

5
Rice, Condiments and Seasonings

A Chinese meal has, traditionally, two distinct components: *fan* and *cai*. *Fan* includes rice, noodles, bread and all cereals, and *cai* constitutes all other foods, such as meat, fish, vegetables, condiments and anything eaten to 'down' the *fan*.

Children are encouraged to eat more rice at the expense of the tasty and more expensive dishes, although a well-prepared bowl of good-quality rice can be as enjoyable as the tastiest of dishes. Today, however, such a bowl of rice is seldom to be obtained in a restaurant, where rice tends to be an afterthought.

The relegation of rice to a lowly place is the result of ignorance and snobbery. A properly cooked bowl of rice should have three qualities: the grains should not stick together, the rice should be soft but resilient, and, above all, it should have a subtle fragrance. For the best results, the rice should be of first-class quality, the right amount of water should be used, and the heat should be reduced at the critical moment and kept up for just sufficient time for the rice to 'cook'. Experience is the best judge. The automatic rice-cooker produces a reasonable rice and it seldom fails; but the best results are obtained by using the traditional earthenware pot over a carefully regulated fire. A crust is formed under the rice, which adds to its flavour and which can be enjoyed on its own. A small spoonful of freshly heated peanut oil or lard and some drops of oyster or dark soy sauce judiciously administered should be all that is necessary to make the queen of cereals the most desirable dish at table.

As the consumption of *fan* is the major part of a Chinese meal, particularly that of the average or poor family for whom meat or fish is a luxury, it is natural that there should be condiments with which to down the *fan*. In northern China it is common for a labourer to have only steamed bread and raw leek for a meal, with some sweet bean sauce as a dip. Southerners are fond of saying that they are content with salted fish and green cabbage to eat with rice. Salted fish, being very salty, is eaten sparingly and only as a condiment.

The multitude of Chinese sauces may also be regarded as condiments. The commonest of all sauces is soy sauce. The light brown variety is known as 'raw' soy because it is less mature. It is saltier than the dark variety which is called 'old' soy. Both are used for cooking and as dips.

Chilli sauce, made from mashed chilli peppers, vinegar and seasonings, is a favourite with the people of Sichuan and Hunan provinces. In small quantities it is very good as a dip for seafood as well as for strong-smelling meat. The fruity plum sauce made from plums, apricots, vinegar and sugar is most suitable for duck and goose. Hoisin sauce, the Cantonese version of sweet bean sauce, is a thick, dark, brownish-red paste which usually accompanies roast suckling pig but which is good with all barbecued meats. Oyster sauce, made from oysters, salt, soy sauce and seasonings, is produced only in the Pearl River delta. Pungent and rich in flavour, it is often used to marinate sliced beef for stir-frying, and as a seasoning for various braised meats, abalone and vegetables.

Chinese sauces, therefore, serve both as condiments and as seasonings. In Chinese cuisine, however, there are many other types of seasoning. Used as a flavouring agent throughout China is five-spice powder, which is most commonly a mixture of star anise, cinnamon bark, fagara (also known as brown peppercorns), fennel and cloves. It has a powerful fragrance, and should be applied sparingly as it is very thirst-inducing. Mixed with fine salt it is also used as a dip for deep-fried foods.

Another common flavouring agent is ginger root, which is

indispensable for removing the strong smell of seafood. Young ginger root is often pickled in vinegar to be served as an appetizer. Mature ginger root has a stronger flavour and its juice is used for seasoning. Ginger and scallion are common allies, and the names of many popular dishes have 'Ginger Scallion' as a prefix.

Popular in Cantonese cuisine are fermented black soy beans which are often used in combination with red peppers. Dried tangerine peel is used both for dispelling a disagreeable smell in an ingredient and also to impart to a dish a special citric flavour. Sesame oil, extracted from roasted sesame seeds, has a strong, pungent flavour much sought after by some but anathema to many. Because the flavour disappears after exposure to great heat, sesame oil is best used as a dressing, applied to a dish after cooking. Serving as a garnish and also as a seasoning is fresh coriander (sometimes called Chinese parsley). It is used sparingly except in the Northern dish of Quick-fried Ox Tripe in which coriander plays the dominant role.

As a seasoning for good-quality stock, Jinhua ham (from the town of Jinhua, near Shanghai) is indispensable as it gives 'body' to chicken stock. Some fanatical chefs, however, go to the extremes of using a whole ham to enrich the stock for a dish of shark's fin. The tender ham will be served intact together with the fin. When a host serves such a dish he is flaunting his wealth and generosity, and guests will show their appreciation by voting with their chopsticks.

6
Provincial Cuisines

CHINESE food is distinguished for its enormous variety of provincial cuisines. However, due to the numerous interchanges amongst the provinces throughout China's history, the origins of many provincial dishes are uncertain. Today many of the dishes which belong to a particular provincial cuisine have become, or are fast becoming, common domain in many of the great cities of the world. For example, Peking Duck, a Northern dish, is served in many Cantonese restaurants; Camphor Wood and Tea Smoked Duck, a Sichuan dish, is offered in a number of Northern restaurants. Of course, many dishes still taste best in their place of origin owing to the force of tradition and the availability of ingredients.

In order to categorize Chinese provincial cuisines, China may be divided broadly into the Northern, Southern, Eastern and Western regions. The Northern region centres on Beijing and extends south as far as the Yangzi River; the Southern region is represented chiefly by the provinces of Guangdong and Guangxi; the Eastern region embraces Jiangsu, Zhejiang, Fujian and the lower Yangzi River basin; and the Western region includes Sichuan, Guizhou and Yunnan provinces.

Generally speaking, Northern food is characterized by a certain robustness, austerity and rusticity. Garlic, spring onion and scallion predominate, and spring onion is often eaten in lieu of meat by the poor, with steamed bread. It is also used as a condiment, and eaten with Peking Duck.

On the topic of Peking Duck an amusing story is told about a miser called Jia. One day Jia felt a craving for roast duck, but could not bring himself to part with any of his cash. At the roast duck shop he could not resist putting his fingers to a fat-dripping, appetizing duck. Having done that he then went home, and licking one finger, downed one bowl of rice; he continued to eat three more bowls of rice in this way before retiring to bed with one finger still unlicked. While Jia was fast asleep, a dog came and licked his finger clean. Discovering the loss when he woke up, Jia was disconsolate, fell ill and did not recover. Such was the deliciousness of Peking Duck.

In the Song dynasty the duck was roasted inside a layer of mud from a lotus pond. In the Yuan dynasty, to cater for the taste of the Mongol rulers, the duck was stuffed with lamb's tripe and other ingredients. Since the reign of Qianlong, a special kind of duck, snow-white, with thin skin and tender meat, and weighing about three kilogrammes, has been used. Today, the duck is referred to as 'stuffed duck', because it is fattened with specially prepared food pellets which are stuffed regularly into the duck's beak. Before roasting, the duck has to be 'blown' to eliminate wrinkles on the skin, coated with barley syrup to produce the dark-brown colour and rich taste, and dried. Traditionally, the fuel over which the duck is roasted is wood charcoal from the date or pear tree.

Mutton Firepot is also a characteristic Northern dish. A good restaurant in Beijing will use mutton imported from Inner Mongolia where the large-tail sheep feed on lush meadow grass, and produce meat which is not only tender but also free from any disagreeable odour. The thinly sliced mutton is cooked in a firepot full of soup made from mushrooms, shrimps and the white of spring onion. The sauce or dip to accompany the mutton is a mixture of sesame oil, soy sauce, red beancurd, sesame paste, rice wine, spring onion and shrimp sauce. At table the diner usually mixes his own dip according to taste.

In contrast to Northern food, Southern food, typified by Cantonese cuisine, is sophisticated, dainty and often exotic. Its three most characteristic qualities are clearness, blandness and freshness. Clearness may be represented by Double-boiled Chicken Soup which should be completely transparent; blandness connotes a certain neutrality in taste, besides moderation in the application of salt, vinegar and spices; freshness refers to the state of being newly slaughtered, harvested or prepared.

Insistence on freshness can make a person go to fanatical lengths for satisfaction. A story is told of the seventeenth-century general, Nian Geng Yao, who ordered his cook to prepare a wok and stove to cook a dish of Stir-fried Pork. A live pig was then brought in, and there and then a slice was taken from its best part and cooked without delay.

Nothing answers the description of clearness, blandness and freshness better than a dish of steamed fish, for example, garoupa fresh from the sea. Properly cleaned, topped with a slice or two of ginger and steamed until just right, the fish has a firm, yet tender, texture. To enhance its flavour, it is necessary to pour over it spoonfuls of boiling chicken stock followed by very hot lard or peanut oil, and finally to scatter over it pieces of spring onion. A simple sounding procedure, but one in which timing is of the essence to ensure that the fish is neither over-cooked nor underdone. Cantonese chefs are experienced at this, and many respectable restaurants have specialists for preparing fresh fish dishes.

To appreciate the subtleties of Cantonese food fully, a description of the dish Chicken in Superior Stock is informative. The ingredient 'chicken' means different things to different people, and choosing the right chicken for the dish is an important part of the procedure.

In Hong Kong, chicken is classified according to the way in which it is used and the price it fetches. Long Gang chicken (from a village near Guangzhou) is considered best, as it has a good flavour, thin, slightly chewy skin and a firmer flesh than that of other breeds. Gourmet restaurants use it for Crispy-skin Chicken and Chicken in Superior Stock. The most popular chicken is 'upper-grade' chicken which is served at banquets because of its good size and tender meat. Qing Yuan chicken (also from a village near Guangzhou) is leaner than other breeds but has a good flavour. *Zhusi* chicken has black skin and bones and is used only to make double-boiled soup. It has an excellent flavour and is the most expensive variety, but is not always available. 'Old' chicken is for boiling and chiefly for soup. 'White' chicken, so called because it has white feathers, is usually lean, with rather 'loose', flavourless meat. Chickens which have been fed or inoculated with hormones are shunned because of their unpleasant taste. Imported chicken is considered the lowest-grade chicken, with a poor texture and 'fishy' taste.

The finicky Cantonese chef or gourmet, having chosen the desired kind of chicken and prepared it for cooking, will have ready a large pot of boiling Superior Stock. Using a ladle, he pours the boiling stock into the inside of the chicken several times (to ensure even cooking), before immersing the whole chicken in the stock. The heat is then stopped, and the chicken allowed to cook in the heat of the stock. This takes about twenty minutes. Stopping the heat at that point ensures that the flesh of the fowl does not contract and become tough. This cooking process is known as *qin*.

The Eastern culinary region favours the original fresh tastes of the principal ingredients. This regional cuisine is often broadly referred to as 'Shanghai food', although this is vehemently contested by the Fujianese who have a rather distinct cuisine which is unfortunately not adequately represented outside the province.

In Shanghai cuisine, sugar is used more generously than in other cuisines. The dish, Smoked Fish, is a good example. A grass carp is cut into pieces about one centimetre thick, which

Flower Boat on the Pearl River, detail, c. 1858
By Tingqua
Hong Kong Museum of Art

New Year Greetings, 1888
By Ju Lian (1828–1904)
Hanging scroll, ink and colour on paper
Height 82 cm, width 47 cm
Art Gallery, The Chinese University of Hong Kong

Bamboo Shoots and Cherries
By Zhang Daqian (1899–1983)
Collection Shuisongshi Shanfang

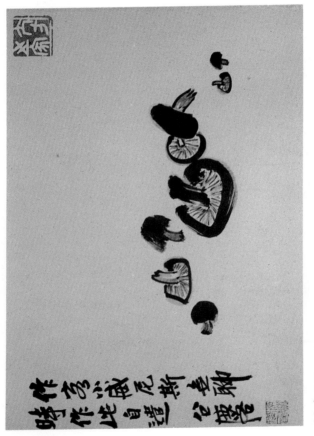

Mushrooms
By Fang Zhaoling (born 1914)
Collection Shuisongshi Shanfang

Autumn
By Chen Qikuan (born 1921)
Collection Shuisongshi Shanfang

Pears Apart
By Chen Qikuan
Collection Shuisongshi Shanfang

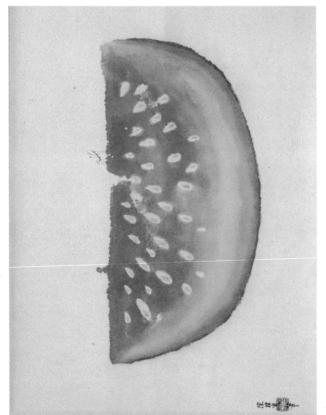

Thirsty
By Chen Qikuan
Collection Shuisongshi Shanfang

Liu Ling, the Confirmed Drinker
By Ding Yinyong (1904–79)
Private Collection

are then marinated for three to four hours in wine, ginger juice, the juice of spring onion and soy sauce. The fish pieces are then fried, and while still very hot dipped in a thick syrup flavoured with five-spice powder. The dish is best eaten cold after the syrup has been completely absorbed. Although it is called Smoked Fish, no smoking takes place, but the taste which lingers on the palate is a slightly smoky one.

A very popular dish in Shanghai restaurants is Stir-fried Fresh Eels, which is served topped with a ladleful of boiling oil and a liberal sprinkling of finely ground white pepper. Another dish which is seldom missing in a Shanghai dinner is the aromatic Drunken Chicken, made by soaking a cooked chicken overnight in Shaoxing wine. One should not leave a Shanghai restaurant without sampling Red-stewed Fish, boiled carp over which is poured a sweetish soy-coloured sauce slightly reminiscent of vinegar.

The cuisine of the Western region is best represented by Sichuan cuisine, which is dominated by the strong, pungent hotness of red chilli, known as the king of condiments. There is a medical reason for its use: it is believed that red chilli expels excessive moisture from the body, thus counteracting the harm caused by the humidity of the climate.

Many Sichuan dishes bear the label 'fish-flavoured', a term which remains a puzzle. The flavouring is not made from fish, but the ingredients of the seasoning were used originally to flavour fish dishes. A dish answering to this description usually has a pleasant brownish colour, a taste suggestive of saltiness, sweetness, sourness and hotness, combined with the flavours of ginger, garlic and spring onion.

Among Sichuan dishes is the famous Camphor Wood and Tea Smoked Duck. A rather dry, spicy dish, it is particularly suitable as an accompaniment to Shaoxing wine. However, perhaps there is nothing more characteristic of Sichuan cuisine than the so-called Returned-to-wok or Twice-cooked Pork. The dish consists of thinly sliced pork, first boiled, and then fried to crispness, flavoured generously with hot red chilli peppers and garlic chives.

7
Home Cooking and Vegetarian Fare

WHERE does one draw the line between a banquet and homely fare? Opinions vary, but in general, dishes made with the less expensive ingredients, such as beancurd, most salted or pickled vegetables, and squid, are relegated to the home. Monosodium glutamate is often rejected in home cooking, but is used in many restaurants to increase the flavour of a dish.

One of the distinguishing features of home cooking is the freedom to invent with inexpensive ingredients. Take eggs, for example. A mixture of one part egg and one part water can be steamed to form a smooth custard known as Water Egg, often with the addition of some tasty ingredients such as dried shrimps, conpoy, minced meat or mushrooms. Eggs may be fried with crabmeat, beansprouts, bamboo shoots and pork; fresh eggs may be mixed with salted eggs and preserved ('thousand-year-old') eggs and steamed to make Three-colour Eggs. The versatility of eggs is boundless.

Beef is seldom served at banquets, except in northern China, but is an important meat in home cooking. Every part of the animal is used: beef fillet is sliced thinly and stir-fried briskly; shin of beef is used for soup; beef brisket is braised but more often used for making soup with assorted vegetables; ox tongue is boiled and seasoned with star anise, cloves and pepper; tripe is boiled for a long time until tender and then dipped in red-pepper soy sauce.

While restaurants produce dishes to be enjoyed by themselves, home cooking aims more at providing dishes to help 'down' rice, since rice is the principal part of a home meal. Thus ingredients that stimulate the palate have a special place in home cooking: preserved eggs and vegetables, preserved beancurd, salted fish, pickled turnip and cabbage, salted plums, salted olives, dried shrimps and various sauces such as oyster, shrimp and plum.

Home cooking is also characterized by a variety of soups which are seldom obtainable in restaurants, except perhaps watercress soup which usually contains duck gizzards (both dried and fresh), freshwater goby and pork. A popular soup consisting of medicinal herbs and meat, usually lean pork, is known as Clear, Supplementary and Cooling as it is thought to have a 'balancing' effect. Lotus roots combined with beef or pork make a favourite soup for the health-minded, as lotus roots are believed to be good for those suffering from mild anaemia. Southern Chinese are fond of double-boiled soups, which are cooked inside a lidded container subjected to steam heat. In this way, the ingredients are not in direct contact with the heat but are cooked under the constant temperature of steam only. Ingredients best double-boiled include turtle, chicken, lamb, squab, teal and dried mushroom, all usually accompanied by medicinal herbs.

The first record of a distaste for the consumption of meat is to be found in the *Zuo Zhuan* (*Historical Annals by Zuo*), written during the Eastern Zhou period (771–256 BC), in which is the statement *'rou shi zhe bi'* ('they are debased who indulge in meat'). However, vegetarian cuisine probably developed in China with the introduction of Buddhism during the Eastern Han dynasty (AD 76–220). Although Buddhist discipline did not strictly require the consumption of vegetarian food, Buddhists would eat only three types of 'clean' meat: that which was not the result of one's own killing, that from an animal not killed at one's own request, and that from an animal the actual killing of which had not been seen. Milk, eggs and fish were considered 'vegetarian' except by one extremist sect.

In his *Xian Qing Ou Ji* (*Musings at Leisure*), Li Yu (1611–80), although himself not a vegetarian, wrote: '... vegetables are preferred to meat for the simple reason that vegetables are closer to nature. The ancients had raiment made of reeds and rushes and ate from plants. They kept away from greasy things and took delight in vegetables'.

Chinese vegetarians have a large choice of ingredients. On the whole, the Chinese are not accustomed to eating raw vegetables, and so most vegetarian dishes are cooked. Many vegetarian dishes are imitations of non-vegetarian dishes, which results in names such as Vegetarian Duck and Vegetarian Shark's Fin. The former consists of layers of thin dried beancurd fried and cut to look like chunks of roast duck; the latter is a thick soup of beancurd shredded to resemble shark's fin. Bamboo shoots, beansprouts, various kinds of mushroom and fungus such as cloud ears, silver ears, yellow ears and hair vegetable, green vegetables and beancurd are the staples in a vegetarian diet. Dried oysters are considered by some to be vegetarian food, but leeks, scallions and spring onions are prohibited from the vegetarian menu because of their strong, pungent smell.

However enjoyable a vegetarian dish may be, it will not have the richness produced by meat. This is borne out in a story about the gourmet, Yi Bing Shou (1754–1815), who advertised for a cook, specifying that the successful candidate would be the one who produced the best vegetarian dish. Among the many applicants was one called Wong who realized how difficult it would be to excel in such a dish. Secretly he soaked an apron in chicken stock, dried it, and took it with him to the test. The dehydrated chicken stock in the apron was then dissolved in the water with which he cooked the vegetarian dish. Naturally the addition of that delicious stock gave him the edge over the other contestants!

8

Exotica

ONE CAN hardly talk about Chinese exotica without mentioning shark's fin, bird's nest and abalone, although these are standard banquet fare and appear on many menus.

Shark's fin is sold dried, and because of the long hours of soaking and cooking required to produce the desired gelatinous texture, the preparation of it is best left to a good restaurant.

Many people are surprised to learn that bird's nest is almost what its name implies. It is the white saliva secreted from the mouth of the golden shrike, a bird which abounds in Hainan and some of the South Sea islands, and is used by the bird to bind its nest. The nest is harvested as soon as it has dried, still full of feathers. When the bird secretes more saliva, this time quite free of feathers, the nest is again taken away. The third secretion, which contains strains of blood, is the most expensive variety but is seldom served at table.

A clear, tasteless substance, bird's nest is best served in chicken stock, pigeon soup or light rock-sugar syrup, in order that its subtle fragrance be enjoyed. To mix it with a strong-tasting ingredient such as crab's roe destroys that quality for which the high price is paid.

There is a wide variety of abalone, a type of mollusc, available in Hong Kong, such as the deep-frozen abalone from Australia, Japan and Africa, which is reasonably priced, and the dried abalone from Japan which is more expensive. Live abalone is seldom eaten by the Chinese. Prices vary: the least expensive dried abalone from Japan is about ten times the price of best beef and the most expensive about one hundred times.

Bêche-de-mer (literally 'sea slug', and sometimes known as sea cucumber) is popular in Northern restaurants. It is a tasteless substance, generally eaten for its texture, and there are two varieties, one soft and tender, the other rather crisper; the former is usually preferred. *Bêche-de-mer* is sold dried or pre-soaked, and after it has been cooked in rich chicken stock, shrimp's roe is often added to enhance the taste. It is sometimes braised with geese's feet or abalone.

Because of its association with the philosopher, Mencius, who lived during the fourth century BC, bear's paw is probably the most celebrated exotic ingredient in the history of Chinese food. Comparing bear's paw to truth and righteousness, and fish to life, Mencius said:

> Fish I love; bear's paw I love;
> If I cannot have both
> I'll forgo fish for bear's paw.
>
> Life I love; righteousness I love;
> If I cannot have both
> I'll forgo life for righteousness.

As it is a rarity and difficult to prepare, bear's paw seldom appears on menus except in Harbin where some restaurants specialize in it. Its texture, after long cooking, is a cross between that of pig's knuckle and *bêche-de-mer*.

The very mention of the name Snake Soup is enough to deter some people who would otherwise consume the concoction with unalloyed delight. Mixed with chicken stock, fine strands of chicken, cloud ear fungus, shreds of fish's bladder, finely cut bamboo shoot and Jinhua ham, the unmentionable ingredient is lost in a medley of goodies. If discovered at all, it resembles tiny pieces of fish. Snake has little taste of its own but adds to the soup a rich, chicken-like flavour. Snake Soup is usually accompanied by small dishes of white chrysanthemum petals, finely cut lemon leaf and a Chinese version of *croûtons*.

Snake Soup is served only between the end of autumn and the end of winter when the reptile is fat and ready for hibernation. Cantonese restaurants often advertise snake with these words:

> The autumn winds have risen,
> The snakes are in good form,
> It's time to nourish yourself.

Traditionally, only the people of southern China eat snake. It is said that almost a thousand years ago, northerners made this scornful remark of the people of Guangzhou: 'Birds, beasts, insects and worms, snakes—they eat them all'.

One of the birds eaten by the Cantonese predominantly is the rice bird. Rice birds descend in their thousands on the rice fields of Guangdong province in late autumn, but where they come from and where they are going remains a mystery. The birds obtain their food from the rice fields, and spend their nights in the reeds by riversides near the sea. They are snared and caught by nets in the evening, often hundreds at one time.

The size of a sparrow, the rice bird has much smaller bones, which are usually consumed with the meat. The most successful way of cooking them is by the process known as *chu*. After the birds' organs have been removed, the cavities are stuffed with a little fresh duck's liver sausage. In a pot, a generous quantity of ginger and spring onion are cooked in a little boiling oil, and then the birds are added, with some soy sauce, wine and a little sugar. After ten minutes' cooking over a good heat each whole tender bird can be eaten in two mouthfuls.

Cornfield worms are another great favourite with the people of southern Guangdong province. When in season, they are available in Macau, where people go specially to sample them. They are usually baked with beaten egg, topped with some deep-fried dough fritters and generously peppered.

Amongst the exotic edible plants in the Chinese gastronomic

repertoire, the least appealing aesthetically is probably *fa cai* (in Cantonese, *fat choy*) which is also known as hair vegetable and black moss. A weed which spreads under some cactus-shaped plants, it abounds in the Gobi Desert but is also grown in parts of Jiangsu, Shanxi, Ningxia, Xinjiang, Inner Mongolia, Qinghai and surrounding areas. Hair vegetable has little taste, but is prized for its slightly slippery texture. Cooked in a rich-tasting dish with plenty of gravy, such as in the popular New Year dish of dried oysters, the hair vegetable acts like a sponge.

A wide variety of fungi are used in Chinese cuisine, especially in vegetarian dishes. Yellow ear fungus is used mainly in vegetarian cooking. Cloud ear fungus, a black variety, features in the Northern dish *Mu Xu Rou*, in which it is stir-fried with eggs, lily flowers and shredded pork. Silver ear fungus, which fetches a higher price than cloud ear fungus, is usually served as a sweet in light rock-sugar syrup.

Chinese inventiveness in the service of the palate is quite astounding. The list of exotic dishes is inexhaustible, whether in the strangeness of the ingredients or in the unexpected ways in which they are prepared or combined. Tea leaves, for instance, may be used as an ingredient in a chicken dish, and ducks' tongues may feature on a banquet menu, as may frogs' bladders or chickens' testicles.

Fashion also dictates new trends in exotica. A few years ago the 'elephant trunk' clam came into vogue. Its texture is like that of conch, but its taste less good. The yak, or horse-tail ox, is considered by some to be tastier than beef, but it is still a novelty that has not yet earned a permanent place on the Chinese menu.

9
Wine and Tea

FROM the wine vessels, long-stemmed wine cups and utensils excavated at the Longshan site in Shandong province, it is clear that China was distilling alcoholic beverages as early as the third millennium BC. The Chinese word *jiu* covers all alcoholic beverages, most of which are distillates of rice, *gaoliang* (sorghum) and other cereals. Grape wine was introduced to China as early as the first century AD, and enjoyed immense popularity during the Tang dynasty. Some of the Chinese alcoholic beverages have the most exotic names: Dragon Flea Tonic *Jiu*, Bamboo Leaf Green *Jiu*, Lotus Flower *Jiu*, Rose Nectar *Jiu*, Double Crab Apple Bubble *Jiu* and Tiger Bone Papaya *Jiu*.

To the West, the best-known beverage is probably *Maotai*, which gained widespread publicity in 1972 when it was drunk as a toast by Chairman Mao Zedong and President Nixon on the occasion of the American President's first meeting with the Chairman. *Maotai* is a strong, aromatic drink, based on millet, and is produced in a town of that name in Guizhou province.

Of equal potency is *Fen Jiu*, which is produced in Apricot Blossom Village about thirty kilometres from the town of Fen Yang in Shanxi province. Voted one of the best strong beverages is *Wu Liang Ye*, which is even more potent than *Maotai* and *Fen Jiu*. In spite of its unusual strength, *Wu Liang Ye* does not go to the head of the drinker. All three strong liquors are colourless although labelled white, and are usually reserved for good drinkers.

A milder drink with the colour of sherry, which is more often served with meals, is Shaoxing (or Yellow) wine, named after the town where it is produced. Made from glutinous rice, it is

usually served warmed, and is used also as a solvent as well as a
supplementary ingredient in herbal medicine, especially in the
making of pills, pastes and powders. It is a custom in Shaoxing
to store a quantity of this wine in the year a daughter is born, so
that when she marries, the wine will be well matured and fit for
entertaining guests on her wedding day.

The Chinese have never been apologetic about an addiction
to wine. On the contrary, many a literary person has glorified
drinkers. The Tang dynasty poet, Li Bo (701–62), was no
exception.

> Bells, tripods, jade and silk are all trash—
> I only wish I were always wine-rapt, not sober.
> The sages of the past are all forgotten now—
> Only the drinkers have their names remembered.

A certain drinker called Liu Ling, who lived during the Jin
dynasty (1115–1234), has been immortalized by this story.
Having downed five gallons of wine Liu fell asleep, and when
he woke up asked for more. His wife reprimanded him for his
excesses, threw away all the wine in the house together with the
containers, and persuaded Liu to give up the bad habit. Liu said,
'Fine. Let me offer sacrifices to the gods first and then ask for
their help. Why don't you go and buy five gallons of wine and
some meat so that I can put them before the altar?' His wife did
as requested and Liu chanted:

> Heaven has given Liu Ling life,
> His name is synonymous with wine.
> I should drink as much as I want:
> The words of woman should be ignored.

With that he drank up all the sacrificial wine.

Although the habit of tea-drinking was in practice in southern China by the Han dynasty, it was not until the Tang that it

became popular both in southern and northern China. Tea was regarded as a thirst-quenching drink, a stimulant and an antidote to drunkenness. Lo Tong, who lived during the eighth century, describes the effect tea had on him:

The first bowl—how soothing to the throat!
The second bowl—all feeling of loneliness vanishes;
The third bowl—I start searching my soul to find five thousand volumes of ancient tomes;
The fourth bowl—a slight perspiration which washes away all unhappy things;
The fifth bowl—my bones and muscles all cleansed;
The sixth bowl—I establish communication with the immortal spirit;
The seventh bowl—this must not be taken,
Already a cool ethereal breeze
Emanates from underneath my arms.

Chinese tea is indissolubly connected with Lu Yu of the Tang dynasty who wrote the first study of tea, the *Chajing* (*Classic of Tea*). Lu Yu stressed the importance of the quality of the water used in the preparation of tea. It was during the Tang dynasty that tea-drinking began to assume the status of an art, which was developed during the Song dynasty to become an attribute of scholars and an accepted practice at the imperial court.

In the Song dynasty and before, tea was made by first pounding dried cakes of steamed tea leaves to a powder. The tea powder was either stirred into boiling water, or boiling water was poured from a ewer into a tea bowl containing tea powder. Many of the early tea bowls had stands to facilitate the handling of the hot tea bowl by the drinker.

The Yuan dynasty saw the gradual change to the use of tea leaves rather than tea powder, which resulted in the method of tea-making practised most commonly today: that of pouring boiling water over tea leaves and allowing them to steep. This necessitated the use of the teapot. In order that the tea might not become too strong, teapots were small and were topped up with water from a ewer.

The six principal categories of Chinese tea (green tea, scented tea, compressed tea, white tea, oolong tea and black tea) were developed during the Ming and Qing dynasties, when the production of teapots and tea accessories expanded greatly to meet the needs of an increasing tea-drinking population.

10

Entertaining and Etiquette

THE influence of Western customs on Chinese etiquette has tended to blur what is typically Chinese. In order to examine Chinese etiquette more clearly, let us turn the clock back fifty years and see what happened when someone gave a dinner party.

If the host was reasonably well off, he would employ a cook and invite his friends to his home. The invitations would take one of two forms. In the first, the details, written or printed on red paper, would be delivered by messenger to each of the guests who were then expected to reply individually. The alternative system was for the host to let each guest know the names of all those being invited. The host's messenger would then deliver to each guest an invitation card listing these names, and each guest would write his reply under his own name. If he decided to accept, he would write 'Coming'; if he wanted to postpone the decision he would write 'Will let you know'; if he wanted to decline, he would write 'Accepted in spirit', and add an excuse if he chose to.

The stated time of arrival was not always adhered to, and the host had to avoid the impression of being over-anxious. When seating his guests the host was guided by their official and social status. If this presented problems, age determined precedence. The host often had to exert much persuasion, not to mention coercion, in trying to seat his guests until everyone had had enough and did as he was told. The seat of the guest of honour was that facing the door, and opposite the host. The next most honoured seat was to the left of the guest of honour.

It is said that the Western host invites his guests to dinner while the Chinese host invites them to eat. There is no doubt that the Chinese take the eating aspect more seriously, and a guest feels at liberty to indulge as he thinks best. He will choose the morsels he fancies from the communal plate, at any frequency, and he will make labial and guttural noises while consuming soup if that is his wont.

A common habit, which still persists in some families, was for the host to serve portions of food to his guests, presuming that they were too polite to help themselves. An over-insistent host could be tiresome, especially if his kitchen was not particularly famous. There was the case of a Changan merchant who loved to entertain but was not much of a gourmet. Once a guest asked him: 'Am I a good friend of yours?', to which the host replied, 'Of course you are'. At this the guest knelt down and said, 'I have one request to make and will not rise until it is granted'. This being agreed to, the guest said, 'Please promise not to invite me again when you entertain in the future.'

Nowadays at many Chinese banquets the position of 'serving' host has been taken over by waiters. The apportionment of shark's fin, noodles or rice is acceptable, but for waiters to serve pieces of chicken or steamed fish is less so. After each guest has waited for everyone to be served, the fish is spoiled, and often a guest will not have been given the part preferred.

A popular form of entertainment between courses or at the end of a dinner is the finger-guessing, or finger-matching, game. One guest first challenges another, and each extends an arm and a certain number of fingers. The two competitors must try to guess the total number of fingers extended. The penalty for losing is to drink the cup of wine provided beforehand. The cup is then refilled and the game resumed. When the guesses of both contestants are wrong, the procedure begins again.

At a home banquet, to ensure that there was enough to eat, or at least that something was seen to be left over, it was customary to have near the end of the dinner a particularly large dish such as braised leg of pig. The symbolic fish was also present. 'Better slight a guest than starve him', says the popular adage, which is reinforced by another: 'In ordinary life, be economical; when entertaining, be lavish in hospitality'.

When it was time to disperse, it was up to the guest of honour to give the cue, and when that was taken, he would stand up. The others would follow suit. This custom still obtains, and is one which often gives rise to misunderstandings on occasions when East meets West.

Woman preparing fish
Drawing from a tomb brick found at Yanshi, Henan province
Song dynasty (960–1279)
Original brick in Historical Museum, Beijing
From *Ancient Chinese Costumes*, Hong Kong 1981

Pottery model of a stove
Late Eastern Han period (AD 76–220)
Height 15.5 cm, length 29.4 cm
Excavated in 1956 at Dayuangang, Guangzhou
Guangzhou City Museum

Kitchen scene, showing game, fish and an oven
Late Eastern Han period (AD 76–220)
Painting on brick from a tomb at Holingol, Inner Mongolia
From *Han and Tang Murals*, Beijing 1974

Servant holding barbecued meat
Painting on brick from a tomb in Jiayuguan, Gansu province
Wei-Jin period (c. 220–419)
From *Han and Tang Murals*, Beijing 1974

Women plucking chicken
Painting on brick from a tomb in Jiayuguan, Gansu province
Wei-Jin period (c. 220–419)
From *Han and Tang Murals*, Beijing 1974

Preparing tea
Woodblock illustration
From *Guwen zhengzong*, Wanli 21st year (1593) edition

Seasonal offerings
Woodblock illustration from a drama
From *Zichaiji*, Wanli period (1573–1619) edition

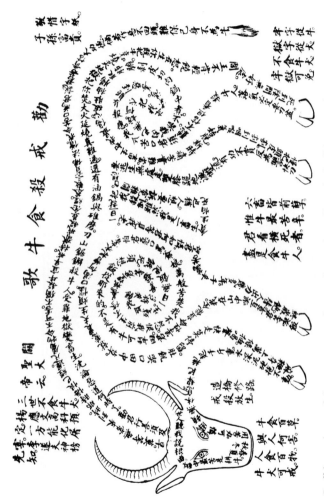

Buffalo made up of characters expressing sentiments including: the buffalo eats only grass and never does humans any harm; it works hard for us, so it should not be killed for its flesh; beef-eaters risk being turned into buffaloes in their reincarnation.

II

Festivals and Banquets

THE Chinese never fail to find an excuse or invent an occasion to have a good meal. The Lunar New Year inaugurates a series of festivities: the first day of the year demands a banquet; the luncheon of the second day is devoted to 'starting the year'; and there are celebrations on the seventh day ('birthday for all') and on the fifteenth day (the 'new fifteenth'). The entire first and second months are suitable for arranging 'spring banquets' at which business firms entertain friends and associates. Formerly these were occasions when friends gathered together to sample new tea and the new vegetables of spring. Spring rolls stuffed with scallions taste best during the New Year period.

In the fifth lunar month is the Dragon Boat Festival, in the seventh the festival of the 'cowherd and spinning girl', and in the eighth the Mid-Autumn, or Moon, Festival. All the festivals are celebrated in one way or another with special food. The 'double-ninth' in the ninth lunar month is the time when people climb up high to rid themselves of bad luck, and is an occasion for feasting, as is the Winter Solstice Festival in the tenth lunar month. Throughout the year there are birthdays, weddings, 'baby-one-month-old' dinners, and many more excuses for celebration.

Ancient history yields few details of royal or princely feasts beyond such bare particulars of protocol as: 'Dukes should be treated to three morning meals and three evening feasts; earls and counts to two morning and two evening feasts; marquises and barons to one morning meal and one evening feast.' The morning meals were intended to be for show only, for 'the wine cups may be full but they are not to be tasted'. The evening

41

feasts, on the other hand, were intended to be thoroughly enjoyed. Participants might 'take off their shoes and drink as much as they could, until wine-rapt'.

The earliest detailed record of an imperial feast is to be found in the *Ming Hui Dian* (*Ming Dynasty Records*). In the thirteenth year of the Yongle period (1403–24) the provisions for an imperial banquet, first grade, included five basins of wine, five plates of fruits, roast chickens, steamed bread and horse-meat rice. Lower-grade banquets had smaller quantities of similar foods.

In the Qing dynasty there were two kinds of imperial feasts: the Manchu, or *Man*, banquet and the Chinese, or *Han*, banquet. As the ruling Manchus were ethnically different from the native Han people, they had a different cuisine. The *Da Qing Hui Dian Shi Lu* (*Qing Dynasty Records and Events*) gives details of *Man* and *Han* banquets. A first-class *Man* banquet used 120 catties of flour, 3 plates of fried cakes, 24 plates of cakes and pastries, and 18 plates of dried and fresh fruits. The second, third and fourth categories of *Man* banquet served similar foods but in greater quantity. A first-class *Man* banquet offered 34 varieties of meat and fruit, a second-class banquet 31 varieties, and a third-class banquet 26.

The first-class banquet was served by the emperor or empress, the second-class by the prince and chief concubine, the third by other concubines, and the fourth was used to entertain important officials and foreign dignitaries. All civil and military examiners were entitled to give *Man* banquets, and according to their ranks were accorded corresponding banquet classes.

The first mention of the combination of *Man* and *Han* banquets appears in *Yangzhou Hua Fang Lu*, a record of early Qing life in the Yangzhou area. The lavish feast of exotic dishes derives probably from the vast culinary experience gained during the tours through China of the Emperor Kangxi and his grandson Emperor Qianlong when the finest ingredients from all over the country were brought together. In the *Yangzhou Hua Fang Lu* are mentioned such delicacies as swallow's nest, fish's bladder dumplings, bear's paw with carps' tongues, gorillas' lips, mock leopard's placenta with camel's hump, civet cat and deer's tail.

Recently, a quaint custom known as dining on 'picture boats' has been revived. Legend has it that while holding a banquet on a picture, or pleasure, boat, Prince Wu of the Spring and Autumn period (771–481 BC) ate raw fish cut into strips and threw into the river what remained after dinner. These strips turned into the tiny silver fish that we know today.

It is recorded that the people of Suzhou and Hangzhou used to entertain in picture boats spacious enough to accommodate over one hundred diners. The mood of the festivities held on board is captured in these lines written in the eighteenth century:

> Suzhou was delightful
> Drinking wine on a picture boat,
> Sampling fine, aromatic vegetables of the season,
> Fresh fish and fowl on bowls of white jade—
> In the twinkling of an eye we reached yonder shores.

Even more memorable were the picture boats in Guangzhou on the Pearl River. The boats were tastefully furnished with blackwood tables and chairs, and decorated with hanging scrolls. The front compartment was for standing or sitting around, the rear one was for dining, and the middle was a study where scholars gathered to compose poems or demonstrate their skills in painting or calligraphy. Some patrons would employ a female entertainer to sit behind them and sing, and to serve dinner.

Cuisine on board was characterized by freshness and nongreasiness. Dishes included Stir-fried Frog Meat, Steamed *Chia* Fish, Tender Beancurd in Superior Stock, Quick-fried Bamboo Shoot with Shrimp's Roe, Congee with Ginkgo Nuts and Silk-sprout Rice from Zengcheng.

12
The Chinese Menu

MANY Chinese restaurants have two sets of menus: a 'regular' one setting out all the dishes on offer, and another listing the chef's suggestions, set menus and foods in season. The former is usually classified under the headings: Shark's Fin and Bird's Nest; Seafood; Chicken and Duck; Pigeon; Roasted or Seasoned Meat; Vegetables in Season; Rice and Noodles; Desserts. As prices of seafood vary according to supply, it is not considered out of place to enquire about the current prices which are usually quoted per tael (16 taels = 1 catty, approximately 600 grammes).

Things to be taken into account when ordering a Chinese meal are the number of persons, the style of the restaurant and the ingredients in season. Unless one is completely unacquainted with Chinese food, one should avoid leaving the ordering to the restaurant staff, who tend to recommend the more expensive dishes and encourage over-ordering. In a Cantonese restaurant the guiding principle is to order one dish per person. Northern restaurants tend to serve larger portions, and so fewer dishes may suffice.

Out of the bewildering variety of a Chinese menu, how does one find one's way? One should aim at a balance of tastes and textures, as well as dietary variety. With this in mind, a typical Cantonese meal for eight may be described.

A meal should begin with dishes which are delicate both in taste and texture and which will not fail to whet the appetite, such as Stir-fried Fresh Shrimps with Bamboo Shoots, or Stir-fried Scallops with Fresh Asparagus. A light second course might be Stir-fried Fresh Mushrooms with Boned Chicken

Wings in Oyster Sauce. It is customary to serve a thick soup at this stage in the meal, and instead of the conventional, expensive Shark's Fin Soup, Double-boiled Whole Winter Melon Soup may be considered, which, despite its name, is best eaten in summer. Diced ingredients such as fresh crabmeat, fresh lotus seeds, roast duck, fresh mushrooms and 'night fragrance' flowers are mixed with a stock made from dried conpoy and frog meat and poured into a partly hollowed winter melon. After hours of double-boiling, the soft, fleshy part of the melon is consumed with the clear soup. Now the diners are ready for something more substantial: a deep-fried chicken marinated in honey, or a roast duck, or a pair of superior soy pigeons. This might be followed by minced quail, pigeon or duck wrapped in lettuce leaves—one of the few occasions on which the Chinese eat raw vegetable. A fresh steamed fish would be an appropriate dish after this. To wind up a meal, fried rice and braised noodles are usually served, followed by a dessert such as Almond or Walnut Purée or a sweet soup.

Because of the abundance of words which sound alike in the Chinese language, much play is made in the Chinese menu on like-sounding words, particularly on a New Year menu. A dish described by the characters pronounced *Hao Shi Fa Cai* (Dried Oyster with Hair Vegetable) is similar in sound to the characters for 'Prosperity and Good Fortune'. Hair Vegetable with Pigs' Trotters, pronounced *Fa Cai Shun Shou*, is similar in sound to a phrase used to wish players success in gambling.

A number of propitious-sounding names are used daily: the sound *ji* means 'tangerine' and 'good omen', *li* means 'chestnut' and 'profit', *gao* means 'cake' and 'high' (thus connoting 'rising'), *yu* means 'fish' and 'surplus' or 'affluence'. In Cantonese, *ha* (prawns) makes one think of 'ha ha', the sound of laughter. *Lian sheng gui zi*, a sweet soup of lotus seeds in syrup, may also mean 'giving birth to a succession of precious children'.

Other considerations govern the naming of a dish: Pork Cubes Stir-fried with Onion simply describes the ingredients; Fish Balls in Hotpot mentions the container; Double-boiled Ginseng Chicken Soup specifies the herb used; Spring Chicken Baked in Mud indicates the cooking method; Peking Duck suggests where the dish originated. Some names require a little stretching of the imagination: Peacock Opening its Wings is a platter of cold meats and vegetables arranged in such a way as to resemble the wings of a peacock; White Jade with Phoenix Claws is a soup with chunks of winter melon and chickens' feet; Beancurd Stuffed with a Hundred Flowers is beancurd stuffed with shrimp paste; and Green Jade and Red Coral is a dish of green vegetables stir-fried with crab's roe.

Suggested Reading

ALTHOUGH many books on Chinese food and cooking have appeared in recent years, most of them contain little more than recipes. One book which confines itself to a discussion of food as an aspect of Chinese culture is *Musings of a Chinese Gourmet* by the late F.T. Cheng (Hutchinson, London, 1954), who prefaced it rather apologetically with this remark: 'It may seem strange to some of my readers that a man after having been a judge of the "World Court" and Ambassador to the Court of St. James's, apart from having held other offices, should on the eve of his seventieth anniversary think fit to write a book on what largely has to do with food and living.' One of the inspirations behind Cheng's book was the remark by the French gastronomist, Brillat-Savarin (1755–1826), that 'the discovery of a new dish does more for the happiness of mankind than the discovery of a new star.'

The Chinese connoisseur and author, Kenneth Lo, has been introducing Chinese food to the West for many years, and his books evince considerable culinary insight. *Classic Chinese Cuisine* (Houghton Mifflin, 1982) is the result of many food tours which the author, Nina Simonds, led to the Far East; *Everything You Want to Know about Chinese Cooking* by Pearl Kong Chen, Tien Chi Chen and Rose Tseng (Barron's, Woodbury, New York, 1983) is a well-researched volume.

An anthropological and historical approach to the subject of Chinese food is to be found in *Food in Chinese Culture, Anthropological and Historical Perspectives*, a collection of essays edited by K.C. Chang and published by Yale University Press (1977). On a regular basis, some diverse and panoramic glimpses of the

48

subject can be gleaned from *Zhong Guo Peng Ren* (*Chinese Cuisine*), a quarterly magazine published by the China Commercial Publishers in Beijing.

Index